THE GOOD,
THE BAD
AND
THE INNOCENT

THE TRAGIC REALITY BEHIND
RESIDENTIAL SCHOOLS,
AN ALBERT ETZERZA STORY

ALBERT ETZERZA

Tellwell Talent
www.tellwell.ca

ISBN
978-0-2288-4179-1 (Hardcover)
978-0-2288-4178-4 (Paperback)
978-0-2288-4180-7 (eBook)

Table of Contents

Inspirations

To the memory of my beloved mother (Mary Una Low) and younger sister, (Rose) whose love and understanding has encouraged me to write this memorandum. To my wife Rose and five boys, (the joy of my life) I trust they will have something I didn't have as a child: Freedom to speak their minds and seek a profession of their choice. May God have mercy on the souls of hypocrites who have negatively affected my life.

sister and brother

Chapter One: Obedience

The first six years of my life were spent in what I consider to be the best of my childhood. Born to a single mother of two small boys, I quickly leant the true meaning of love. We were a close-knit family. Because food was scarce, my mother decided to register us in school away from home (residential). Little did she know the devastating effect this institution would have on our lives.

At the age of six, I was thrust into a routine of prayer and sexual molestation. The residential school preached prayer and penance. The hypocrisy of their attitudes was overwhelming. Not only was there constant beating for childhood antics, but the system attracted people who molested young children. They had complete control over First Nations.

At an early age, I quickly leant to excel in school and to submit to the molesting, which was very prevalent. We were taught that Natives (Indians) were lower than second-class citizens. Our existence on earth was solely to be taught by white superiors. The meaning of a (white) civilized world. This meant total obedience to their every command and inhuman needs.

Can you imagine thinking beatings are justified and molesting normal just because they were initiated by these so-called holy people? Did they really think that God would automatically forgive their wrongs because they were the messengers? If this was the way they thought, are they ever going to be surprised in death. God did not ok all the molesting; it was human error, issued on a pair of mitts and a jacket in winter that we had to make sure we didn't lose. Those who lost mitts or a jacket were sent out anyways. The weather was usually 20 °F and sometimes dropped to -40 °F. Those who ran away (which was a frequent occurrence) were shaved bald.

Further punishment consisted of a public strapping in front of the entire student body and staff. The strap was leather, approximately three feet long, three inches wide, and a quarter inch thick. This was meant to cause much pain. The students were lined up with hands extended. The principal (priest) always did the deed. If the boy pulled his hands away, he was given extra. I can vividly remember the priest being exhausted from all the hitting. His red face will always remain in my memory.

Watching this torture has affected me, and I am sure the rest of my Native sisters and brothers. My feelings are neutral, as I am not militant to the point of hate. I sometimes break down in tears but do not hate these people. At the same time, no love is projected. I have love, but it is well camouflaged by projecting no feeling.

obedience was taught in the school

Where

Where have all the good days gone?
They've faded into the past
Where have all the good days gone?
They were short and fast

We like to relish the good old days
Many would just as soon forget
We like to relish the good old days
I sometimes sit and wonder
Why days seem longer

Where have all the good days gone?
They've faded into the past
Where have all the good days gone?
They were short and fast

Remember when you smiled
Try to focus on that thought
Remember when you smiled
It was the end of a drought
We can rely on happy times
To make our past a distant memory

School

Where have the children gone?
They were here yesterday
Where have the children gone?
They were taken during the day
Did they really have a choice?
I see no one in rejoice

The tears that are shed
Are tears of sorrow and woe
The tears that are shed
Are not false and do not flow
But rather pour relentless
Resisting is powerless

They herd us in trucks like cattle
The cold winds of fall sting
There are too many to cause a rattle
We huddle close to avoid the fall wind
You see we had no choice
What is there to rejoice?

Chapter Two: School

As I left the sunny skies of Tahltan, my soul descended into a massive cloud, which has not cleared since. My two older brothers (eight and ten) had no idea that our innocent lives were about to change forever. Accompanied by Mom and our younger sister, the ride from Tahltan to Dease Lake seemed like a lifetime. My only memory of that trip was the car sickness I felt in my stomach. I was not punished, as my mother was present. I entered the system in the fall of 1951 and didn't get out for any summer vacations until June of 1957. Six years without a breath of fresh air. What did we do to deserve this?

My mother thought it was a dream come true. Not only were her children getting an education, but she was hired as a baker in the newly built residential school in Lower Post, B.C. She was approached by the Indian agent and priest with a promise of being there with her children. As we would obtain a much-needed education, she relented. She later told me that the happiness of not being separated from her children was more than she could hope and pray for. Her employment was short-lived. A year later, she was terminated because she was not the baker desired. To save money, it was the policy of this particular school to leave out certain necessary ingredients. This left the bread heavy and Mom refused to bake bread, which she said was barely edible.

My mother moved to Prince Rupert, B.C. and we lost her presence at the school. It was two long years before we saw her again. We, along with a few other students, were forced to spend the summer months confined in the residential system.

For whatever reason, I've come to understand that poverty was why our mother could not take us out of the residential system until that year. She saved money and made a special trip from Prince Rupert to spend a couple of weeks with us. She rented a cabin and took us out for two glorious weeks. All too soon, she had to leave. Holding back tears, I soon broke down in a fit of sobs as my older brother cried.

I will never forget the words my supervisor said to me. He said, "I can't understand why you have any reason to cry. After all, you have me." In his twisted mind, he actually thought that his weird ways were what I was looking forward to.

I longed for a normal life. Hugs and kisses were not normal. Long gone were my mother's presence and kind words to guide us in our childhood years. Of everything that happened, I mostly missed the hugs and kisses, which were so prevalent from my mother. When we did see her, it seemed she couldn't get enough of hugging and kissing us.

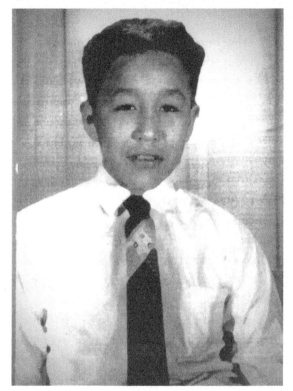

Age 10

MOM

I had a dream last night
She came to me in all her might
Her face was so clear
She seemed so near

Through all the incidents occurring
Her smiling face was assuring
I temporarily lost the pain
That seemed so in vain
I now can face the day
As dawn comes without delay

I had a dream last night
She came to me in all her might
Her face was so clear
She seemed so near

I thank God for mother
So serene and kind
It wasn't any bother
I fall asleep to find
Fortitude in life once more
I know for sure she is the core

mother and son Albert

Chapter Three: Language and Culture

The children in this northern residential school came from various tribes across northern B.C. and the Yukon Territories (Tahltan, Kaska, etc.). The missionaries had one thing in common: to produce white replicas from "savages." To this end, we could no longer speak our native language amongst each other.

The main focus of our education consisted of religion, religion, and more religion. I suppose their job was considered done if, above all, we had a religious background and believed in their god. We were not allowed to speak our native language or spend time reminiscing about Native culture. Nice try! Anyone caught speaking First Nations was punished by strapping. Who was the "savage?" If speaking our language continued, we were forced to wear girls' clothing as well. Do you wonder why we grew up ashamed of our cultures and languages?

Out of this group, statistics say that between sixty to eighty percent of residential school children were alcoholic. I say this figure is totally wrong. My true belief is that one hundred percent of us are alcoholics. Many of us are now non-drinkers but never-the-less alcoholic. As we grew older, it became evident that residential influence had a lot to do with our odd lifestyles. This conception is strong. As we pass blame, we wallow in pity and despair. Too many former students have lost their language and culture.

Steps have been taken in that direction. Some day, Natives will have books written in tribal languages to pass on to future generations. To be proud of one's culture, one has to speak openly about languages. I wasn't the only one to have suffered the loss of both language and culture. We don't have to camouflage our feeling and capabilities. To say, "I'm proud to be First Nations," is not enough. We have to prove beyond the shadow of any doubt that progress has been made. Time to stop talking. Time to take action.

Participation in all Native events is a must. Too many times, events are slated but with minimal attendance. Our children have laid the foundation; Elders should sit up and take notice of the strong will they possess. Think about it and take positive action. I can see dances and ceremonies coming back. Elders teach these almost-lost ceremonies, but it takes more than teachers. The younger generation is willing and excited to be taught by Elders. Our children are like light in a tunnel. I am proud to see them perform and carry tradition to future generations. We've started a spark and it has grown into a flame, which will never be extinguished. They are the fuel who will keep the flame ignited forever.

Wonder

Is it any wonder that I got drunk?
Is it any wonder my heart sunk?
Did I drink to forget?
Did I ever regret?

The booze seemed to ease
The pain and release
Memories I'd rather forget
And live a life of regret

I used to live in a shell
It was pure hell
With no place to turn
While my insides burn

Chapter Four: Friendship

The main focus in their thinking was not to encourage friendship amongst us. To form a friendship simply meant a plot against the core of religious domination. But like all other efforts, it failed. True, many boys and girls became loners in a shell of their own world. To escape the cruelty of not associating, I formed a special relationship with two other boys. One has since passed on to greater reward. The other has very successfully gone on to become a man of God (different religion).

This friendship was cut short one night in a pedophile's pleasure. He wasn't satisfied with one boy, so he got two of us in his room for personal use. This time he had us performing acts of disgust. He sat and watched us performing acts of sex on each other. I was ashamed from that day, well into my adulthood.

It all changed in court. Our testimony helped send this creature to prison for thirty plus years. Having gone through the court process against the church, government, and individuals, I do support reporting sexual offences. I must warn any future participants in such a predicament to keep an open mind. Number one: do not approach charges with hatred. Always have support personnel around your group from day one. Fortunately, we did have such support. Our support showed up at court and thereof. I trust all future groups will secure support people as soon as disclosure.

I must stress at this time that as children we were not responsible for our actions. Too many brothers and sisters are led to believe they were the ones responsible for what was done to them and their bodies. I, to this day, do not completely trust another man. Time heals all wounds, (misconception) but understanding that there is good in all people helps. Faith in humanity, faith in a supreme being, are like two peas in a pod. Having that helped me to achieve faith in people again.

Albert and his friend

Albert and his friend

Dawn

How often I've seen the dawn
Without the fawn
How often I've awakened
To find I've been forsaken

I go to sleep
And hope for peace
I have no place to keep
I cannot find the peace

I know not when my turn will come
I close my eyes and pull for sleep
Which never seems to come
I try to drift into the deep
Is it any wonder?
I seldom slumber

Chapter Five: Abuse and Cover-Up

The happiest times during my long stay were seeing my mother once a year after the first two years. Also, getting to know all the other children, especially when school year started again. Seeing my friends meant a lot.

I didn't realize it at the time, but this also slowed down the molesting. I now realize that he was also doing this to other boys. This meant he had less time for me. This particular supervisor even stayed during the summer holidays with approximately eight boys. Therefore, he had more time to concentrate on us.

It seemed like a daily happening during that time. How I longed for the third week in August each year. Why was this allowed, especially when this was reported by two brothers (in approximately 1956) to the parish priest?

The priest showed up that year with the boys in tow. They were brought before the principal and told in no uncertain terms that this matter was closed. Amen to that! We had nowhere or anyone to turn to. Even the RCMP were notified, to no avail. These words were used in conversation: "For the sake of the Catholic Church, we must keep this quiet." What a blatant cover-up. All attempts to reveal beatings and molestation were put to rest bluntly. This was a Roman Catholic Church cover-up in conjunction with the RCMP. I say this of the two boys during the course of our trial.

Subsequently a retired policeman came forward to aid in our monetary settlement with the government and church. I, for one, did not report a molesting until 1990, thirty plus years after the fact. Due to the graphic nature of their actions, I was totally ashamed to let anyone know what had happened.

Also being brainwashed took its toll on my conscience. Although my body knew what happened, my mind was not about to admit to any wrongdoings until that day in 1990. Knowing I was not the only one molested brought more credence to my statement. Thank God for the courage of one man whose conscience would not take any more reminders of past years.

My memories of movies are vague. I think we saw them once a month. These movies were not Academy Award winners, except for the religious ones. Most of the B-rated movies were about romance or were Westerns with violence. The scenes depicting physical contact, such as kissing, were covered up. The Westerns and others, displaying shootings and killings, were shown in their entirety.

Is it any wonder that bigger boys became bullies? The staff were not the only ones to watch out for. Our own Native brothers preyed on smaller and weaker ones. Here again we dared not tell, or else. I remember standing up to another boy who was older and bigger. My brother was coming to my aid. Through tears, I told him not to help. I took my beating and kept on ticking. I fought back, to no avail. Years later, I stood right beside him in our court case against the system.

I really can't think of any other words for the residential schools except for what they really were: jails and concentration camps. Certainly, no love, understanding, or family attitudes were projected. The Catholic Church used these as a money-making scheme to further enhance their financial empire.

Summer

Summer is approaching
Time for my friends to go home
Summer is a time for loafing
It makes me feel alone
My friends are gone
I'm left alone too long

The days seem to last
The nights are in the past
Why does the touching happen
More often? I know not why
I wish my friends could come back
The touching would become slack

Where did I go wrong?
I have to be strong
I'm looking for a cure
I have to be sure
The privilege to forgive is mine
I have to focus on this line

Chapter Six: Religion

From day one, the main purpose of our incarceration was focused on religion. We had prayers when we woke, before breakfast, after breakfast, before classes, after classes, before lunch and supper, and also after lunch and supper. To top it all off, we had to pray before we went to bed.

Saturday afternoons were spent going to confession for all the sins we were told we had committed. All who went to church were expected to participate in Holy Communion. We were watched constantly but expected to be sinners. Consequently, we had to go to confession and receive Communion on Sunday. Every Sunday we had special clothes to wear for mass. It probably was the same in all residential schools. My confession was basically the same every time. I would confess to having dirty thoughts and my penance would be reciting the Rosary.

I didn't mind praying then, and to this day I still pray daily. I didn't lose my belief in the Catholic Church, although I attend church on a very irregular basis. I also do not force my boys to attend church. Basic belief was installed by my mother (bless her soul). She was religious right to the day we lost her to cancer.

Humans (priests, brothers, and nuns) took advantage of religion to not only force their misguided beliefs on us but also to be hypocrites by also molesting us. Most First Nations children were not as fortunate as I was.

Throughout all this turmoil, my belief had been fortified by my mother's regular attendance in church and by living a life of honesty and love for her children. Her religious conviction was so strong that I believe it is now projected in my daily life. I try not to let a day pass without thanking the Lord for my family (my wife and five boys) that I have. I pray, giving thanks for what we have, not for what the "Jones" have. I am human and I do pray sometimes for things we don't have.

I can remember as a small boy that my mother prayed for food, which was scarce. It seemed as if her prayers were always answered. Some person would show up at our isolated home, thirteen miles from Telegraph Creek, with much needed meat. I can't dispute the fact that they showed up when we needed meat.

To err is human, but to forgive is divine. I still have a long way to go. I first have to try to understand why. We were children whose privacy was invaded by religious people, to satisfy their lopsided needs.

The diocese bishop was stationed in Whitehorse, Yukon. It seemed like a million miles away. We actually looked forward to his periodic visits, particularly on religious holidays. Those were special occasions for us. A big front was put on. We were dressed to the best of Indian Affairs' standards. He always had a special mass.

As a young child, I can remember the day was spent in awe looking at this religious figure. They had us convinced that a mere mortal was supernatural. Another thing I constantly heard about this particular person was his love of children.

I don't believe he was totally ignorant about the evil actions his staff had participated in. His pat answers on earth will hold no credence when he passes on. Does God have a special place reserved for his kind? He turned his back on children he professed to love. His attitude must have raised hell on his conscience. He did nothing to stop the beating and molesting. In human terms, that is lying to the utmost.

All this was done to further enhance the Catholic Church. Is it any wonder that this sect is one of the riches entities in the world? It came down to dollars and cents— building the church at any cost, even human lives, which were forever affected by these schools.

Throughout all this, God's presence has remained in my heart. Maybe someday, through prayer, I will completely forgive their evil ways. I may never understand why they did all this to a particular group of people. I do know the evils of this world will be answered for in the hereafter. We were put on the earth to project love amongst each other.

I've leant that we can hug and kiss without sex being involved. Basically, we were taught that to show love, sex had to be involved. That is the perception given to us as children. But without love we are just lost entities. I've progressed to the point where I can show love without sex. After all, we should not be ashamed of our sexual activities with loved ones. True love comes from a person's heart, as well as their body. The weird tactics used on us must not be a model for our actions towards future generations. We must treat our children with respect as well as love. After all, one follows the other. Love is nothing without respect, just an empty shell. This is the greatest gift we could pass on to our children. Children are lovable as well as trustworthy. If we could keep our childhood qualities, the world would progress into a tranquil and peaceful utopia.

We, as a nation, have to progress to our former being. This means reverting to the methods used by our ancestors. In this way, we will not only treat our children differently but restore our self-respect.

Survivor's Lament

Dream O Freedom
From these walls of confinement
I dream of freedom
From these walls with no sediment

We the children of innocence
Live in a world of prayer and penance
When we analyse the teacher of democracy
All that's left is hypocrisy
They teach you how to pray
But with you they lay
As our hopes turn to despair

I dream of freedom
From these walls of confinement
I dream of freedom
From these walls with no sediment

Where has it gone?
We slowly lose our faith
And search for answers too long
Is there a quick fix for mistrust?
That causes all this pain

Chapter Seven: New Supervisor

The year was 1955 and we, the children of residential life, were about to meet the ultimate molester. It was common practice for the nuns to parade in and out of the boy's residence whenever. I can remember watching the sister superior standing in the shower doorway. She would stand and watch us shower, in particular the older boys. Did she get her sexual kicks this way? Who knows? She does!

The fall of 1955 dawned, and we all had the same thoughts: The new supervisor was sent from God. He came to the residential system with a firm mind that no nuns were allowed to approach our dormitory section. We praised him for his actions. Little did we know what was to come.

It started innocently, just like a concerned parent. After we showered and dried, we were told to line up outside his room. One by one, we entered his room. I couldn't understand what was happening to me. I was told to drop the towel around me. Completely naked, I was also told to approach him. Looking over my body, he fondled my penis to the point of erection. Being ten years old at the time, I didn't know what was going on. Now I know for certain that he was picking out boys for his personal pleasure. At the time, he made me feel his private part. At my age, I was curious; I didn't know it was only the tip of the iceberg.

He apparently singled out numerous other misfits for molesting. His approaches were made mostly during the night, during his nightly bed checks. He would stop at my bed and motion for me to go to his room. From simple touching, his actions soon proceeded to ejaculation. He made me jack him off. I can remember the smell of a male body and ejaculate. For the longest time, it almost made me puke. As I got used to the smell, he progressed to kissing and putting his tongue in my mouth. I was also forced to take his penis in my small mouth. The final straw was an attempt to enter my rectum. At this time, the pain was too much, and I cried out. Fortunately, he stopped.

Those memories are sick, and I will never forget them as long as I live. I don't think his kind have any conscience. He was the one to remark that I didn't have anything to cry for when my mother left.

"After all you have me."

His mind was pretty twisted to think he could replace my mother. If only I had confided in her at the time. I know she would have believed me. But in a world dominated by priests and religion, it might have been to no avail.

The brother who reported incidents to their parish priest didn't even get acknowledged. We had to wait thirty years for any results. Society would like to acknowledge and say, "I know what you went through." I say bull! They didn't experience anything that happened. Sympathy is entirely different than being a victim. I have a hard time talking, but it seems easier to write. I am just writing about my life, years ago, and what kind of hell it was. We survived, but our minds and bodies suffer still. Yet life must go on. I would like to speculate that my writings will benefit other survivors of what happened and, in many respects, should never have occurred.

We've leant to go through life teaching our children about love and under-standing. The beatings we endured cannot be projected and used on our loved ones. When we say the buck stops here, we have to include our actions in that statement. Talking means nothing. To get positive results, we have to fill those empty shells with love and understanding. Too many times a statement is just that, a statement. We've progressed to talking, and it is time to start putting this in our family values. Sometimes it seems easier to get results by hitting and screaming. But calmness has a much better effect. We forget that our children are vulnerable, being easily misled by our actions. Children can be perfect clones of parents.

We've leant as First Nations people that being degraded doesn't necessarily mean total disaster. By following our forefathers' example, we can start treating our children in the proper way. Our lives are projected by future generations (children and grandchildren). Future misfits are not what lies ahead. We must strive to correct all we've been taught as survivors of residential discipline.

If we love our children as much as we love ourselves, then we have to project it in everyday life. If a child looks in the mirror and visualizes their parents at their side, then we are on the right track. The phrase, "I love you," should never be looked upon as being used too frequently. All children do not talk through their hats. Projections of love are pure and come from sincere hearts. Didn't we at one time or another wish we could remain young forever?

I think that as a child who had no say in daily activities, it made me bitter and headstrong. I went along with residential routines to avoid punishment. Their types of punishment did not justify mere child antics and minor mishaps that occur in everyday life. The justification of being there was not enough to justify punishment. Even to the point of molesting small ones.

I really don't know of anyone who did not relent to any approach which involved sexual touches or more. But in the back of my mind, I often wondered why some were beaten more than others. Could they be the ones who actually said no? Did I do wrong by relenting? As an adult, I must say that guilt was a big issue: being a young child and having those actions performed on me. They singled me out. I wasn't the only one in this predicament.

Being brainwashed by submitting us to witness strapping, etc., had its effect on me. This certainly had its effect on the outcome of our future. Through healing over the last ten years, I came to accept the fact that I can forgive. But will I ever forget? I still have to comprehend why and how. I saw no remorse from this person during court procedures. He still said that he was sent to the school to take care of children. Although I realize that forgiving is a start in the right direction, they, as adults, are responsible, certainly not us as children. No responsibility was taken on their parts.

Through out my long stay in residential school only two people molested me. A psychologist would have done the staff a favour by intervening. But would it have done any good? Their thinking would have remained the same. They somehow justified all methods and procedures used. Talk about the ends justifying the means. The staff would rather hit a child instead of finding out the reason for misbehaving.

I now can compare my confinement at this school as a jail sentence. The problem being, we did no wrong and still served time.

Bitterness was a major setback to the majority of First Nations escaping the system. This included alcohol, drugs, and total disrespect on our part towards females of our clans. Our ancestors had the greatest respect for female members of the clan. They were revered and listened to. That has altered since Columbus "discovered" North America.

These were some examples of abuse leant from childhood. This is a reason, not an excuse. We didn't have any method to deal with the opposite sex. Many are not satisfied with one partner; cheating is common. All this is done without merit because any excuse was viable to us. If we can't blame our partner, then why not the system?

I've started to learn how to accept responsibilities. I got tired of putting blame on the past. Time to look forward to raising my children properly and living a normal life. This is easier said then done. I still have a long way to go. Writing about my past helps.

I sometimes wish I could go to sleep and wake up a different person. That method has no reality. It is only an easy way out. Wishful thinking! The world is a challenge, and all incidents are part and whole included. I am dealing with this one day at a time.

Any nation degraded to the extent of First Nations could sit up and take notice. I believe we've set an example for the world to observe. Everything humanly possible was taken from us: our customs, beliefs, languages, etc. We were mistreated and humiliated as children, yet we survived. They would have succeeded if not for the strong will we possessed. They destroyed bodies but not spirits. Over the years, our spirits survived, even as our bodies could take no more.

The greatest accomplishment out of the residential schools is our forgiveness. A lot of us still have to learn to understand. For this we do not require a psychologist's point of view. Our Elders' voices were heard beyond the beatings.

This reminds me of a preacher who came to our apartment. He came to convert a few more souls for this religion. After listening to his remarks about love and understanding, I had my say.

I said, "You sure have nerve coming to me with your love and so-called understanding. You first came with the Victorian era attitude of mistrust and belittlement. When you found out that humans thrive on principles deeply embedded by our ancestors, you've changed your mind. Do you realize that your basic principles now stem from our true beliefs about our existence on Mother Earth? You beat our beliefs out of us, so you thought! Now you stand before me to tell me what I've had in my spirits all along. We have our own teachers for that. Our Elders! Go preach to someone else. Amen!"

No matter what I said, this man found excuses to justify his mission on earth. His final words were, "How could you blame present clergy for incidents that happened before my time?"

There again blame was passed on to an earlier generation of religious instructors. A person who has been through the system and survived could have many negative sides. The danger of passing on negative aspects is a possibility. The worst aspect would be an elected official, such as a chief. If he is a survivor and has not disclosed or forgiven, then would he, in essence, be guilty of passing on residential school values to tribal members? Pretty scary. The possibilities are too real of this likelihood. How do we safeguard this not happening? There are no real safeguards, but educating our people by word of mouth, meetings, etc., is a proper procedure to start with.

We have to share this knowledge with all our people, or else be prepared to face continual residential treatment amongst present and future generations. Our people have not lost the ability to learn, although control of our emotions was one of their top priorities. I must say, success was too close for comfort. Thank God our free will is controlled by other realities, ourselves. No matter what, we still control our own minds. That can never be taken from an individual. We can fake our emotions but willpower comes from a higher entity. It is not issued to certain individuals. We all possess this marvellous ability. The world would not last long if we did not have this precious gift. We would become puppets controlled by a few individuals.

We've certainly come a long way since residential closures. I have lived to see a governor general who was First Nations. I trust someday Canada will see fit to elect a prime minister who is truly Canadian too. Too many times I've heard, "How could this have happened to Natives across Canada?" Well it occurred, so we have to face these issues head on.

In days gone by, we were powerless to report or do anything because cover-ups were done at all costs, even human dignity. The dawn of a new era has begun.

The Lord said, "Forgive them for they know not what they have done." The sad part in that statement is the fact that they did know what was happening. It was a cover-up for various reasons. To this day I do not hear any owning up to any incidents. What we hear is different from the truth.

Forgive

I love to sit and write
Especially about my plight
It seems to ease
And aids to appease
Whatever the past signifies
And hope it identifies

Do we have to carry the burden?
Or can we learn to forget?
Does the planting of a garden
Carry any regret?
If we have one thing in common
I hope it's forgiveness

Forgiveness for the wrongs
Thanks for the parent
Forgiveness for the wrongs
Let go the past and relent
To thoughts of serenity
And thoughts of family unity

Chapter Eight: Kidnapped

As I've mentioned previously, God would not send messengers to molest and be cruel to children. Basically, we were fed and clothed. This statement justified excellent providers, in their estimation. Natives also got a much-needed education. What I've written is proof of that education. Remember, at sixteen, freedom was taken by almost one hundred percent. The few remaining students progressed because of free will.

In June of 1959 I was elated, as my next school year I was moving to Whitehorse, Yukon (grade 9). That summer I was going to Prince Rupert for the holidays. My fourteenth birthday had just passed, and it was great, as my two older brothers had previously gone to Whitehorse.

Smithers, B.C. was a normal stop on the way to Prince Rupert. I was three hours away from seeing my mother again, this time for the whole summer. As I sat waiting patiently for the train to pull out, I noticed a former supervisor with a conductor approaching me. To my surprise, I was told to stay with this man. My heart sank as I obediently followed them off the train. I didn't know what was going on. The man said everything was ok, my mother had told him it was all right for me to stay with him.

First of all, how did he know that I was going to be on that particular train? Little did I know that through communication with the principal of the school that I had just left, all this information was given to him. He covered up any charges of kidnapping after the fact, by writing to my Mother, assuring her that I was going to be properly taken care of. At age fourteen, I found out that nothing had changed, he was still up to his old games. All the brainwashing had paid off for him. I was still obedient to his every wish and weird way.

This time he took advantage of my body every night. When Mom finally contacted this now social worker, the cover-up began. He had previously written a letter to her explaining his intention of sheltering me. He also had a job waiting for her. She came and worked there for approximately two weeks. After that, she moved my younger sister and I back to Prince Rupert. He had taken advantage of me for the last time, so I thought.

I spent a wonderful summer with my mother just being a child once more. On my way back to school in Whitehorse, he was once again waiting for me in Smithers. The residential system had hired him again.

We stayed in Dawson Creek, B.C. I was subjected to another night of submitting to his pleasures. That was the final night of being shamed by an adult. The memories of intrusions on my body will never be forgotten.

I tried to charge him with kidnapping, along with all those other molestations, but to no avail. The judge threw out those particular charges. The law works in mysterious ways. What I said was considered second-hand information. This didn't hold any credence in a court of law. My younger sister had explained to me in detail how this particular incident had taken place. My memory of that time in my life is very vivid. What I didn't know was that Mom did not give anyone permission to take me off that train. I call that kidnapping. The judge said I was told about Mom's initial intention. This does not cover up the fact that this man took me without permission. Here again, the law protects the guilty. My satisfaction in the incident was his imprisonment, although for other crimes against me. Due to his age, I hope he spends the rest of his natural life behind bars. I, for one, could not detect any remorse from him for his actions.

Fears

The fears we had are real
They stem from years gone by
The fears we had are real
We will face them with clarity
We will face them one by one
We will solve them one by one

We've leant to solve our problems
One by one, it took courage
We've leant to solve our problems
One by one, with effort we had to forage
For strength to attain

It seems my fears are gone
Has the past dissolved?
It seems my fears are gone
With this thought I'm resolved
To contest this storm
To solve, rectify, and reform

Chapter Nine: The Move

The fall of 1959 was a special time in my childhood. I was going to grade 9 and Whitehorse. I joined my brothers who were in grades 10 and 11 respectively. I had looked forward to this moment for two long years. I relished every childhood day spent with them. We were boarded out in a place called, Maryhouse. Hence the name "Maryhouse Boys" was tagged onto us.

This particular place was for vagrants of the Yukon. Operated by Catholics, it was basically a Salvation Army institution. We were subjected to further humiliation by being placed in this below-standard living quarters. This served as another roadblock in efforts to complete grade twelve. Also, the sudden change from a totally Native school to public was drastic, to say the least. The hardest part was adjusting to mingling with kids of different backgrounds.

The inferiority complex I felt was just another weight and burden on our efforts to finish schooling. I can remember many humiliating incidents the first year in public school. I found it harder to succeed in classes where prejudice was prevalent. I soon found out that it was common practice to be belittled in public on a daily basis.

Nothing was ever done about those unfortunate insults. Many times, I felt like giving up, if not for my brothers.

I was introduced to a whole new way of life socially; even the dance was different. Sports, like basketball, were new to me. Can you imagine? Previous to this, I had never seen a basketball. I didn't know a thing about the game. Our innocence and ignorance were obvious and used to other students' advantage. Slowly we jelled in with the rest of the student body. I eventually leant, liked, and progressed into a fair student.

That first year's experience was just like science fiction, except it all occurred. I look back on this time in my life as a major growing-up period in my successful graduation. I give thanks to the Creator for providing our family with a mother who stood by her family with love and no alcohol. To this day, I know we had an advantage over other Native kids. We had a parent who gave advice and also listened to our questions. If this was done in residential systems, there would have been more students who succeeded in graduation.

I really can't imagine systems at the time operating with the principles that Mom projected. Living through years of confinement would have been so much more pleasant and family-like. If not for reservation laws that prohibited employment off-reserve, our parents would have had the resources to keep Native children at home. We can't argue the fact that First Nations drank to excess. Being confined in an area with no chance of employment does something to your spirit. If a Native dared to work off-reserve, then Indian status was revoked. Reinstatement didn't happen until a few years ago. Therefore, means to support families were limited to trapping and virtually nonexistent. Downhearted fallings were left, along with easy access to alcohol. Most drank to forget and ease the pain of unemployment. I don't know what reasons or excuses were projected by laws like that.

How does one address this situation? Life in the system can be described as unbearable, but we survived. We survived to tell the story of an injustice done to a human race. Injustice that can never be resolved by any monetary endorsements. I know, as I've gone through the justice system and received what was perceived to be retribution in the form of dollars. One can argue: how will money wipe out the memories? It doesn't, but forgiveness helps to ease the pain and nightmares we now endure. Nightmares that still persist after forty plus years. I am only one of thousands taken, sometimes by force, to live in prison-like atmospheres for the sake of money, in my estimation. Money, because the Indian Affairs and government paid for each child apprehended. More Natives meant more money.

Let's put all nonsense of making better citizens out of "savages" aside. If they were trying to make better humans out of us, why all the beating? Even dogs are not obedient after a trashing unless they were continuously beaten. Methods of public strapping were common in all residential schools as far as I know. Watching these beatings served a double purpose. We all knew what was in store for us if we dared to disobey. It became obvious even after being molested.

We didn't dare talk about those affairs. A friend of mine was told as a five-year-old that the molesting was all his fault. How can a young mind handle an accusation like that? This does something to your mind, and I am talking about guilt. Guilt on that five-year old's mind.

After holding this inside me many years, the truth came out with a force which is not explainable. I have no hatred for ignorance but being told, "I understand what you've gone through," releases a new form of anger. How can you understand if it didn't happen to you? The scars left behind are not healed by understanding. Neither are they abolished by saying, "I'm sorry." That burden is carried, unfortunately, by First Nations, sometimes to untimely deaths by alcohol and suicide. We've carried the burden. Mostly guilt for atrocities done to our childhood bodies.

I've often thought, what would have happened had I said no? Would I have had to face retribution by being beaten? Therein lies the guilt. As an adult, I now know what happened was inexcusable. As a child, I had no choice but to submit. Children are sometimes helpless to adult influence. This somehow eases the pain and memories. I know memories will always remain and healing takes time. Life is too short, and we must somehow move on.

I've heard through media sources that Canadians have listened to First Nations' complaints enough. They say, when is it going to stop? I have news for the ignorant statement. It will never stop. I agree the blaming of alcoholism and suicides are responsibilities we have to carry, but the stories should never cease. Responsibility is two-sided. All we require at this junction in life is understanding. Understanding that it takes time to release the animosity towards the race responsible.

I don't hate, as many others, but in reality, feel sorry for someone who thinks they are superior because of colour and creed. Equality is stressed in schools, to no avail. How come that throughout all schools, Natives are still not up to par as far as the education standards are concerned? There seems to be two standards, one for Natives and one for other racial groups. It is sad to ponder these facts of life. We have to fight for recognition and still be looked at with pity.

Even now, my thoughts are that reserves should be abolished. The only purpose they serve is superiority. We don't have any say or choice on size or even where a reserve is situated. We are given land that is rightfully ours to begin with.

Yesteryear

O'er faded memories of yesteryear
My wants and needs fade like distant drums
The sounds become less
I try my utmost best
To erase all negative feeling
That surface to leave me reeling

I'm left alone to face the impact
Without trust that I lack
Praying for understanding and endurance
I'm left without assurance
Assurance that I know true love
Assurance to fly like a dove

Even as I understand love
I cannot fly like a dove
But love and understanding
Make me feel love notwithstanding
All the past wrongs inflicted
All the past wrongs directed

Chapter Ten: Hockey and Highschool

Hockey season came, and I found a meaningful purpose in my teenage life. I was an excellent skater, like most First Nations, and the possibilities were unlimited. Discrimination was very prevalent in 1959. There were numerous hockey teams in Whitehorse, but two were comprised of First Nations.

A year before I came to Whitehorse, our team, CYO, had only one non-white participant. He too was a reject from other teams. He donned thick glasses and other teams would not consider him for any position. One day, we had no goalie, and he was asked to fill the position temporarily, as we didn't know if he was eligible because of his nationality. He became a regular. Eventually he became the most valuable juvenile goaltender in the Yukon.

That year, in 1959, our team went undefeated during the regular season games. The "Maryhouse Boys," as we became known, captured every available trophy offered in juvenile hockey, including the coveted Goaltender Award. After a successful season, we entered the playoffs full of confidence, maybe too much. The first round was a breeze;

we went undefeated again. We were in the playoff finals. The position was also comprised of First Nations. They presided at a local Indian mission school. We entered the playoffs full of pep with thoughts of sweeping this team.

We ran into a brick wall. The first two games were history, and our team was down two games to nil. Entering the third period of the third game, the score was 6-4 for the opposition. The coach came into the dressing room peeved from our lack of performance. He motioned to the utility line to sit down. He then focused his attention on the rest of the team. He angrily said that our line was the only one deserving a rest. We didn't score, but we were not expected to, but no goals were scored against us either. The rest of the team was told to stand the whole intermission and look at us for good examples of how to play hockey properly. We were quite nervous having the stars of our team looking at us for ten minutes.

The third period produced four goals, all ours. We went on to win the rest of the games and take the juvenile championship, once more showing team spirit. I was proud then and will always be proud to be a member of a team comprised of mostly First Nations.

The other extraordinary aspect of this special team were the five sets of brothers. It was truly a family affair. I was the youngest and smallest member of that team. It all seems like it happened yesterday. I must mention that our goaltender used a softball catcher's mask during practice and this carried on into the league games. I believed he started using the mask a year before I came (1958).

Our team was comprised of a nearsighted goaltender and the rest had virtually no regular hockey equipment.

We just used what we had. We eventually went on to win the most valued prize in juvenile hockey. Our team won, not because of talent but sheer tenacity. We always believed in our abilities and skated together with confidence and for the pure love of hockey. Life was never boring in Whitehorse again and I progressed in my education as well. I went on to captain several winning teams, but that year was a landmark in my entire life. It felt good to prove that we belonged and also dominate an aspect in my young life.

When I finished grade 10 in Whitehorse, I thought I was finished. I told my mother that I wasn't going back to school in a place run by a religious sect that dominated us. I really meant that I was finished with residential schools. My two older brothers had graduated, and I was determined not to be isolated again. In her wisdom, she agreed. My actions almost cost me any further education. That summer, I was lucky to secure a job in an asbestos mine in Cassiar, B.C., along with my older brother.

After working for two months, I was ready to enter a public school. This time, the move to high school in Prince Rupert, B.C. proved too much for my unstable mind. I missed the entire month of September 1962. I started late because the entire month of September was spent drinking up all the money I had made during the Summer. At first, I had thoughts of getting another job. There were no jobs available for an inexperienced seventeen-year-old.

Mother came to my rescue once more. She paid my bus fare, and I was again back in school. This time I was in for an even bigger shock. I was totally on my own for grade 11 and being a month late didn't help. My biggest problem was alcohol. The school year was like a dream as my main focus was partying on weekends. This usually carried on well into the next week. This happened a lot and I found myself approaching my younger sister to forge absentee notes.

The frequency of these events made it impossible to keep up. I was slated for another failure. I had already failed grade 10. To my utmost surprise, I passed. I know that the teachers passed me just to get rid of me. I passed on subjects I'd only attended for one day. I didn't feel good about that year. I was entering grade 12 with minimal knowledge.

That summer, I was approached by Mom with an idea of going back to a boarding school. I knew that success was within reach under these circumstances. The school was open to all denominations regardless of religion or creed. I was now eighteen, but I had taken the opportunity to go back to a boarding school. My grades soared to a new level. I realized success was not impossible if I settled down to a year of studies and hard work.

This time I graduated in the top five in grade 12. I was also chosen as the salutatorian of Prince George College Heights (1964). The emotion was overwhelming while preparing a speech with my mother present. I was offered a drink to celebrate the occasion, but I refused. My mother's example was good enough for me. My speech was also flawless. I didn't read from notes. I had memorized four pages. Graduating with excellent marks was a dream come true.

At this time, I must mention how close I came to not even going beyond grade 10. During my second attempt in grade 10, I was called into the principal's office. I was told that I was taking a course in heavy duty operating. When I questioned their choice, the answer was blunt: "I'm afraid you are not going to pass your grade again."

When I questioned his remarks, the priest put his hands together in prayer and said, "We know these things." I later realized the reasoning behind this statement. I was seventeen and a year older than the age Natives usually attended school. This was surely a cop-out on the education of First Nations. He said I was one of three lucky ones chosen. I refused. The priest said I was wasting everyone's time by continuing school. I proved them wrong.

My two older brothers' graduation had a big influence on my decision to continue. A decision I never regretted. As I was told to quit wasting school space, I angrily said, "Father, I could pass my grade without studying." I did pass.

This time I had gone against their principles with my decision. I knew this wasn't going to end here. It was the end of the school year and all students had gone home. I was called to the office for a final time.

He said, "I have a good mind to kick you out of this system because of your negative influence on the students. You're one of two students that have caused turmoil over the last year."

I told this priest that I didn't give a damn, as this was my final year in residential school. What I didn't say was that I had no intention of quitting school. He used his influence to hold up the southbound Greyhound bus. They waited an hour to accommodate my departure from residential life. They had just proven that education was secondary. I had stood up to their authority, and this meant my departure was necessary. I wasn't wanted to influence other students. So be it! Rather than admit they were wrong, I was used as a bad example. My influence wasn't wanted in their one-sided system.

In that short span, I grew up. I had made a decision and I wasn't influenced by brainwashing. The ghosts of residential superiors were gone. In the back of my mind, I laughed as my relationship with these individuals was over.

I didn't go back to Whitehorse for another twenty plus years. My memory of those days was fresh in my mind, as one day in 1986, I drove the 350 odd miles back. This time I was going to watch a Native hockey tournament. It was a good feeling to meet old school chums after a long self-imposed absence from the Yukon. People don't change, only time. We were all older but pleasant memories still existed.

This made me realize that through all the miseries and molesting that happened years ago, I could still pick out the good times. Times that helped me make it through all the years spent in residential schools. We made friendships in those years, which also aided in surviving hardships. Religion had a sole purpose in life. To liberate souls for its flock. We were part of that movement. The methods they used were cruel and hypocritical.

We used every means available to survive until the age of sixteen. My brothers and I were some of the few that continued school after that age. In fact, we all went on to graduate. Watching them graduate helped me through my ordeal. I had leant that education was important, to succeed later on in life. My mother played an important part in that decision. From the time we were old enough to understand, she would tell us to take advantage of the education offered. She guided us through school from afar. Although we didn't see her, sometimes for two years, the letters didn't stop.

From an early age, I noticed that she didn't drink just to get drunk. This habit, unfortunately, was very prevalent amongst Natives. Instead, she would occasionally have one beer with my relatives. After that, she always had reasons not to have any more to drink. I drank to excess too long. After twenty plus years, I finally quit. I will always be an alcoholic, although drinking is the furthest impulse from my mind. I did follow her example after all. It's a good feeling to know that a tiny woman could have such a big influence on my life. I know now that the success and education I attained was a direct result of my mother's life and good examples. From a very young age, I can remember her words of encouragement. They came directly from her heart.

One aspect of my life that she did not pass on was hatred. She had no room in her life for hatred and lies. The residential school taught us to lie and become hypocrites. As adults, we the survivors must take positive notice of our ancestors. Their true grit and wholesome honesty are trademarks for us to follow. They were a proud people. Salvaging their attitudes must be a First Nations' priority. Life must go on but with positive thoughts on our part. We must take back the values and everyday routines our ancestors possessed.

Love of our children must replace meaningless beatings. How we react will surely influence the future generations of First Nations' attitudes of rearing our children. We must realize that a young child also has a mind of his or her own. I don't think that forcing them to attend church or other activities will make for better citizens. When they do attend church with me it will be because of free will. Until they truly understand and appreciate the presence of a superior being, they should be left alone to play. After all, we are children for only a few short years. I was made to kneel down in front of a human being and ask for spiritual forgiveness. Forgiveness for what? For being a child? Our childhood antics were magnified into sins.

To me, those people not only tried to take the place of our parents but also tried to act the part of God. Did they not know our innocence as children were the values which would count in the here after? If we remained children for life, the world would become another paradise. Guided by our ancestors' lives and beliefs, we would progress in a more positive way. Simplicity in life must be adhered to. The hustle and bustle of life is not necessary to survive. Keeping up with next door should not be a priority. The competition of being better financially should not matter. The rich will inherit the earth but the poor the heavens. Life on earth is just a steppingstone to a greater reward.

A lot of my residential imprisonment was spent dreaming of life beyond those walls, which seemed impossible to penetrate. My whole childhood was taken from me. I didn't grow up normally, I just grew up in a world where there was no love. I mean that in the residential system nothing beyond school boundaries mattered. The inferiority complex was prevalent, and we found ourselves becoming like whites just to survive. This avoided punishment. I really can't speak for others, but I believed that I was only one of two that was being molested at that time. They were so good at molesting that it seemed as if they went to a special school to learn how to molest.

One might argue, how could we not know about the others? The strategies used worked one hundred percent. No one dared talk about activities done by this maniac. They brainwashed us, put out the fire, but left a small spark. A spark which slowly came alive over the years and eventually started burning again.

Being as good as the next person in life is very important to me. They do not have to come from any specific race or creed. I believe we, as human beings, are all the same. Throughout my tenure with First Nations, I noticed a lot of prejudice from our side too. There again the system triumphed once more. Since that time, I hope our people can live normal lives without prejudice and hatred.

Learn to live in harmony without prejudice. Love your children and respect will follow, especially the female sect. Our women play a large part in the success of all tribes, as was done centuries ago. Today they are still the driving force in any tribe in North America. We seem to forget that our existence from day one of conception depends on mothers worldwide. The first nine months we are completely dependant on their nourishment to stay alive and remain healthy. After birth, once again, we are the main focus of our parents, especially mothers. Our mothers become more personal, as being fed from her body is a connection we have for life. The love I received the first six years cannot be erased by years of adverse treatment. This was done by residential superiors and staff. We underestimate how the abilities and power that mothers have affect children.

In a normal family, the child has the advantage of a mother's love and understanding in their early years. Most Native children were taken from parents by the age of six. I was in that category. But the early years are etched in my memory. Mom's influence aided in surviving the residential years.

All this love was not realistic in those schools. As I mentioned, activities were not oriented towards rearing children normally. No hugs or kisses were ever used, only discipline. Our opinions were never heard or heeded.

I was once asked by a prominent doctor, "I fail to see the difference in our white children being molested in boarding school, as compared to First Nations in residential schools."

I said, "With all due respect, doctor, you paid to send your children. We were taken illegally."

Some children were taken without parents' consent (kidnapped). Others, like my brothers and I, were sent because the priest offered Mom a job for as long as we attended. Her influence and strong will were too much for them to handle. After one school year she was let go because her baking was not up to standard, so they said. A certain ingredient was left out just to save money. She knew of only one way to bake bread, the proper way. They got rid of the one person whose closeness and love would have made our stay at the institution bearable.

I would like to point out that the molesting started even as she was working there. This particular person could only think of his personal lopsided needs. I can still remember that a few days after entering Lower Post Indian school, a brother took me to his room. This was done during the day. Later, after the first encounter, my obedience took over. The pleasure was all one sided—his. After all, I was only six years old. I was still too young to comprehend what was going on. Also, the stench will always remain in my memory. A memory I would rather forget. At the time it seemed so normal, but at the same time I dared not tell anyone about what just happened.

dads team

ice rink

brothers

ice rink was very hard to skat on

dad's hockey a. etzerza presented with the juvenile
championship trophy for the winning 918 team

HOCKEY

The world's fastest game ever played is exercised on our rink at Domano. Both the Juvenile and the Midget teams have a wonderful coach in Brother Kearns.

In actual fact, hockey is not an easy game to play. First, you must be able to skate exceptionally well; secondly, you must learn to control the puck. Because the game is so difficult, our team must practice often. They go to the colosseum twice a week; Monday, from 6:00 A.M. until 7:30 A.M. and Thursday, from 7:00 P.M. to 8:30 P.M. They also practice on their own rink whenever possible.

The Juveniles play against teams in such places as Burns Lake, Fort Fraser, and Vanderhoof.

The spectators were gratified to see that our teams were exceptionally well mannered.

Douglas Morris '65

school hockey team

60

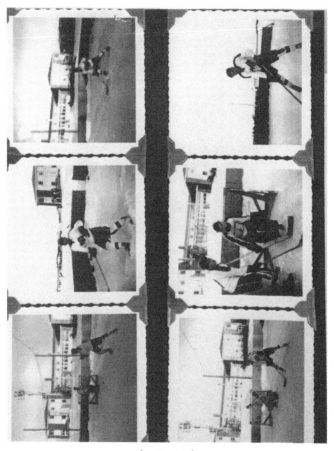

skating rink

grad day

grad pin

ORDERS OF THE DAY FOR GRADUATION

1. Processional - accompanied by Mr. Thomas -

2. O Canada - STAND

3. Invocation - Most Rev. Bishop O'Grady - STAND

4. Choral selection - "Let There Be Peace on Earth" - SIT

5. Salutatory - ALBERT ETZERZA - SIT

6. Conferring of Diplomas by the Bishop - STAND AND PROCEED TO THE
   STAGE AS YOUR NAME IS CALLED. RETURN TO YOUR PLACE AND REMAIN
   STANDING UNTIL ROW IS COMPLETE; THEN SIT TOGETHER.

7. Valedictory - BARBARA GUNN-FOWLIE - SIT

8. Class Pledge - To be led by PAULETTE DE GRYSE from the stage - when
   she reaches the steps all STAND. SIT as she comes down the
   steps.

9. Choral selection - "He" - SIT

10. Address - Rev. S. Gordon, O.M.I., Pastor at Smithers, - SIT

11. Greeting to Graduates - The Bishop - SIT

12. The Queen - STAND

13. Recessional - accompanied by Mr. Thomas

THE ORDER OF PROCESSION IS ON THE REVERSE SIDE ALONG WITH THE ORDER

IN WHICH YOU WILL BE PRESENTED FOR YOUR DIPLOMA.

he was the salutatory at his grad

Albert Etzerza

Maryhouse Boys

The annals of time have changed
But my memory is fresh
We took to the ice and changed
Forever the concept we were less
Remember days of yore
That happened before
Laws prohibited discrimination
We skated as a nation

We reached the pinnacle
Of any team's effort to win
We achieved the impossible
We knew when to begin
And didn't play to lose
Although we savoured no booze

Release the pressure
That causes all this uneasy feeling
Take back your assurance
That leaves us reeling
We've spent some time on top
Will that feeling ever stop?

Maryhouse Indian Boys Win Hockey Championship Again At Whitehorse

For the second year in succession the Indian students of Maryhouse at Whitehorse have won the Juvenile Championship of the Yukon. Going undefeated all winter, they captured the league title for the second year in a row.

Victorious in the semi-finals, they lost the first two games of a best 3-of-5 series with the Baptist Indian Mission team, then came back strong to win the final three games and the championship.

The Maryhouse boys began playing hockey in Whitehorse for the C.Y.O. team, and eventually became the only members — with the exception of goalie Dave Carter, the only non-Indian on the team.

There are five sets of brothers: Richard and Jackie Carlick; Joe and Alfred Chief; John and Danny Johnny; Vincent and Joe Dennis; William, Belfry and Albert Etzerza. Philip Joe, who joined the team late in the season, has two brothers who will soon be old enough to continue the tradition.

Coach A. H. "Robbie" Robinson developed these boys into players with a splendid team spirit.

Maryhouse Champions — Back row, left to right: Albert Etzerza, Jackie Carlick, Joe Denis, Danny Johnny; middle row: Vincent Denis, Belfry Etzerza, Coach "Robbie" Robinson, Alfred Chief, Philip Joe; front row: Richard Carlick (captain), Dave Carter, Joe Chief, William Etzerza (high scorer of the league).

Albert hockey team Maryhouse native boys win hockey championship at Whitehouse

Chapter Eleven: Food

The food served was not fit for a dog, who will eat anything. Below are a few examples of our diet.

Breakfast:

Usually breakfast every day consisted of porridge. Mostly farina or rolled oats, the porridge was always lumpy and undercooked. Sometimes we got pancakes.

There again the centres were mostly raw. During my confinement, I can remember getting an egg once a year at Easter. We were issued only one boiled egg. The superiors always made mention that we should be extra thankful for this extra gift from the religious people present (the priests, brothers, and nuns). On Sundays we were treated to puffed wheat. We had tea to drink.

Lunch/Supper:

A lot of this was served half cooked. Boiled barley with no additives was the main dish almost every day and I had difficulty consuming any amount. We had barley boiled with not even salt added. Have you ever eaten boiled barley with not even salt added? I almost vomited many times eating this particular food. To this day, I avoid barley, not even putting it in soups. We had white fish, cooked the same way. Most of the time we were fed meat that was spoiled. All this had to be eaten, or else. We were served bread that was not properly baked, ingredients missing.

Tea to drink:

Tea was usually served as a beverage on a first-come basis. As there was limited amount of tea put out, the motto was, "The ones who drank the fastest got the most." I only have to close my eyes to remember the mad rushes for extra tea. There was more available near the kitchen. Each table had two servers for approximately twenty students. I can still remember servers from each table running around the table with tea and rushing to get more. The first ones got a chance for maybe a third pitcher. This was unreal.

Dining:

As we entered the dining room from the boys' side, we had to pass by the staff's eating quarters. The door was purposely left open; their meals reminded me of a banquet. The serving pots were made of sterling silver. Roasts, pork chops, turkeys, etc., steaming with vapours, drifted into the hallway. We were told not to look as we passed. We could see what they ate and just wished.

Right after that, our goods had to be consumed. It was garbage compared to what they ate. This part always reminded me of the Oliver Twist movie, which they showed to us. Every effort was made to save money by feeding cheap scraps, only to have to force feed us sometimes. Food was eaten, or else. We always had reminders that our food was provided by the grace of God. Hence, we had to pray before each meal. As messengers of God, were they entitled to more than us? This sort of thinking is backwards.

I can remember mealtimes as a madhouse. I would classify the actions as panic. There was a lot of rudeness and shoving during meals. I would say that mealtimes at the residential school taught us to put aside table manners.

In 1959, the principal died, and a new priest was appointed as guardian. The first thing he did was to make a big show of eating with the students, with a sole purpose in mind. He wanted to get the trust of all students. He ate the same food as us and, for once, we got food that was edible and properly cooked.

The problem with his gesture was that it only happened once. The next meal, we were served the same garbage, which was a routine. That meal became a memory. As children, we were both surprised and delighted by his actions. We thought, here was someone who really cared, but we never saw him eating with us again. After that, he showed his true colours.

That same summer, two brave boys reported their molestation to a parish priest. This particular priest brought them back to school personally. At the school, a meeting was arranged with the principal immediately. The outcome of that meeting was silence for another thirty-five years. They got their chance to talk when charges were laid against the school, government, and individuals involved. This time, they were free to speak their minds. And they took advantage of court procedure. This time the charges prevailed. That priest will not see the outside of the prison walls in his lifetime. God works in mysterious ways and we are thankful for the opportunity to speak our minds.

We were free to tell about incidents that happened to us so many years ago. Negative feelings have faded but, by the grace of God, my memory after forty plus years is vivid. It is with this vision I've put together facts and truths. I have no reason to add Hollywood effects to anything written. Telling the truth is easier. Because one lie leads to another, I've relied on my memory, which, in my estimation, is very dependable.

Time

As I while away the time
In my sanction of refuge
I think about days of yore
I'm not so sure
Whether the right they taught
Was all done for naught

I sit about and try to think
On time spent on the rink
Practising all the skills
Not worrying about any bills
You see we had none
We were so young

If thoughts could become reality
The past would be more clear
If thoughts could become reality
I'd prove to anyone who desires to hear
That our childhood life was harsh
Living it again would be a farce

Chapter Twelve: Laundry and Showers

Saturday was laundry day, and that morning was a busy one, as we stripped beds and gathered discarded school clothing for washing. All bedding, etc., was put in a laundry shoot, along with everyday clothing. Laundry was done by the female students. The washing of school clothing was infrequent, and I really don't recall whether they were washed once a week or every two weeks.

On Sundays, we donned white shirts, slacks, and shoes. The white shirts were washed every second or third week. Slacks and shoes were put away for the week. The slacks were washed only once a year…chores were probably imitations of Canadian prisons.

We had no privacy, only the peering eyes of government employees. Sisters (nuns) came up beside us unexpectedly, even when we took showers. I often wondered if they got their sexual satisfaction in this manner.

After showering, inspection was mandatory, instigated by a certain supervisor. For this we had to be naked. This was, I presume, his opportunity to pick out victims. Touching all parts of our bodies, the supervisor saved the genital area for last. What happened here was not for medical reasons. Fondling private parts seemed to excite this supervisor.

Later, I was summoned to his bedroom after the rest of the boys were presumed to be asleep. The molesting had begun. After that, it seemed as if he had a schedule to follow. I was only one of numerous victims. I'm sure his actions repeated on as many young students as humanly possible.

I blame him for the deaths of my brother because of alcohol and drug abuse. I myself lived that life until a few years ago. Many of us have still not, and maybe will never, recover from these addictions.

Return

You took my clothes
You took my hair
You gave me your clothes

You took my language
You took my basic belief
You gave me anguish
Which wasn't a relief

I have taken back my clothes
I have taken back my hair
You can keep your clothes
I know that's only fair

You seem to forget
About my regret
You seem to forget
I live not for regret

Chapter Thirteen: Working Chores

Each child was assigned a daily chore with major clean up on Saturdays, according to age and abilities (which they decided). Our duties were listed military style. We searched for our name, number, and specific job for the week. The dirty jobs, such as cleaning the washrooms, were given to those deemed to deserve less meaningful tasks.

There was no consideration of age. If a child had an accident in his clothes or bed, then he spent extra time on latrine duties. There was a certain boy whose main chores during his confinement were only bathroom cleanings. He had a habit of wetting his bed.

On Saturdays, main chores were done, such as scrubbing all areas (dining room, bathrooms, etc.). After completion, each job was inspected by a superior. Incomplete jobs were not tolerated. It had to be done again, but this time a toothbrush was used. They had a saying, "Some kids never learn." The third time was strapping time in front of the rest of the boys. Believe it or not, they seemed to take pleasure in using the strap to get a point across.

After the strapping, we were once again made to complete the job. After a while, I began to notice more chores being done right the first time. I heard, "You see, you can complete your assignment properly the first time." It was done their way to avoid punishment and humiliation. We were brainwashed; there simply is no other explanation.

Is it any wonder we didn't learn to accomplish anything in life without punishment? A high percentage ended up in jail soon after leaving. What other life did we know of? Some deliberately committed crimes just to end up in a similar place they had just left and loathed. I drank alcohol to numb the brains to blackout stage. In that state, I didn't have to answer to anyone.

Many times, I woke up in jail, not knowing why I was picked up. Police picked me up many times because I was so drunk, I was beyond coherence. Going to work for a month or two became a cycle.

I was told, "You are not an alcoholic."

I still found work as I drank to excess. Little did we know that alcoholics are in many classes and stages. I still looked forward to the next drink as I worked. I always drank for the same reasons. I actually saved money to drink without depending on someone else to buy my booze. We've been misled too long. It is time for a positive change. Living as an alcoholic becomes normal procedure for all residential school survivors. I lost some jobs for the love of alcohol, not because I was lazy. I cannot recall all the times I've said, "Never again," meaning I wasn't going to drink again. It was a never-ending story.

To all survivors of residential abuse, just remember that to gain sobriety you have to start living your life as yourself, not as drunks and with violence. Since the closure of the last residential school in the 1990s, we have changed our thing. It took that action to trigger a response in our everyday living. It also took one brave man to step forward with the truth. The healing had started. We now can focus on the future and look back at our negative past with the knowledge that we are not the ones responsible.

As children, we did not have the physical strength to resist. The physical abuse led to mental as well. This is not mentioned in any brochures that I've read. Methods of silencing us worked one hundred percent. So we entered life with a weak perception of right and wrong. Many First Nations faced charges against children, which copied actions from years gone by. We are still responsible as adults, but now we have found a reason for our actions. These reasons do not justify wrongs committed by First Nations against children.

Why

I know not why
I only know how
I stand before a looking glass
And see a glimpse of my past
It is a person I see
Not someone that used to be

The power to change
Is within my range
Therefore, I know not why
I only know how
The past remains the same
The future is like a game

We've survived our holocaust
What more can you ask?
Living this ordeal was at a cost
We can now take off the mask

Lives have been taken
Lives have been scarred
Healing is on the horizon
Is forgiveness too far?

Chapter Fourteen: Weekends

We rose at 7:30 a.m., made beds, washed, and said prayers. Breakfast was at 8:00 a.m. with prayers before. At 9:00 a.m. Saturday morning, we had major clean up. A special chart was put up, listing everyone's chores to be accomplished that morning. All floors were swept and scrubbed to perfection, or else. Walls were washed spotless. Anyone not doing their chores to residential standards was given treatment accordingly.

After completion, the lucky ones were free to play outside until lunch. At 12:00 p.m. was lunch with prayers, to thank God for all the good food before us. Then we had to consume all this food, which was considered slop most of the time. This was very hard to eat, especially for those who had weak stomachs. Fortunately, most tables had one or two cans labelled, "garbage bins." They basically ate the goods we couldn't.

Punishment was forthcoming to all who had the nerve to dispose of what was classified as gifts.

1:00-5:00 p.m. was considered free time for all those who completed their chores satisfactorily. This time was spent in the school yard, except for occasional hikes. I believe most of the hikes we took were on Sundays.

Sometimes we even had meals cooked by senior boys. Those times will always be cherished in my memory. It meant being out with Mother Nature where we all felt at home. Those times were used by most of us to shoot small game with sling shots (grouse, rabbits, etc.).

I would say that our generation was classified as experts with this deadly toy. More often than not, we killed a few grouse and the occasional rabbit. This game was supposed to be brought back to the main camp for the supervisor. Most of the grouse was cooked and consumed in hiding. I know this because the group I hung out with very seldomly brought anything to the main camp. It was times like this that helped us survive the system.

All too soon we had to get back to the school for supper. Supper on weekends was probably served at 6:00 p.m. Occasionally, we were late. When that happened, we faced punishment. It was usually worth the extra freedom. The outdoors seemed to relieve the feeling of being closed in for another week or so. At supper, we once again said our prayers before the meal. The supper was usually served with tea. As mentioned previously, meat was served, sometimes spoiled. We somehow didn't die from all the germs and sickness emanating from the meat.

Destiny

Many times I've wondered
About the life I've led
Many times I've wondered
Why I haven't given up and fled?
I only know now
What I didn't know then

Life is no simple task
Life is a complicated mess
How can you ask
When you know no less?
I have a feeling to triumph
Did I really beat this slump?

The world is brighter
As night becomes dawn
My load is lighter
Just like a mowed lawn
I've lived to see the light
Darkness does not become the night

Chapter Fifteen: Monday to Friday Routine

7:00 a.m. Awaken and pray before making beds and washing up.

7:30 a.m. Breakfast with prayers before eating.

8:00-8:45 a.m. Each student do their specific chore before classes.

9:00 a.m.-12:00 p.m. Prayer, classes, prayer.

12:00-12:45 p.m. Prayer, lunch.

1:00-3:00 p.m. Prayer, classes, prayer.

3:15-4:45 p.m. Free time, except for those being punished.

5:00-5:30 p.m. Prayer, supper.

5:45 p.m.-7:30 p.m. Chapel, free time, and bedtime for juniors (6-12 yrs). Showers, prayer.

8:30 p.m. bedtime for seniors.

Nighttime was when most of the molesting was done. The supervisor would make a point of checking all boys in bed during the night. I didn't notice, and thought I was the only one being molested. He would come to my bed and just tap me for the signal to go to his room. Little did I know, there were many others. So many that an officer taking my statement said, "This man must have been superhuman."

The fifteen trail blazers that testified against this man were only the tip of the iceberg. Since that time, numerous survivors have stepped forward and accused him of the same crimes committed against us. A pedophile has a routine, which is repeated. Selection of victims becomes easier as routine becomes regular. He had a schedule in his mind, which became a reality. All victims were chosen, most likely, after showering. That was the reason for the inspection of our bodies for whatever. All this man was looking for was a reaction of any sort from small children. His kind will always be remembered as the lowest point in the incarceration of First Nations, Canada-wide.

Some of us took it harder than others, and many refuse to admit that any wrongdoing was ever done. Of course, we in our minds and souls all know that what he did was wrong and we pray for those who refuse to acknowledge.

Past

Whatever happened to the past?
I'm so glad it didn't last
We think of memories
To aid us through the days

If apologies are measured in dollars
Let's go out and holler
An apology in words
Make us feel like lords
After all is money everything?
Or does it add up to nothing?

Whatever happened to the past?
I'm so glad it didn't last
We think of memories
To aid us through the days

How do I stop this feeling?
My head is reeling
I remember the forlorn past
Memories I hope don't last
The words to apologize
Do not synchronize

Chapter Sixteen: Reasons we Entered Residential School

Mom's husband passed away, (1942) leaving her with nine children to raise alone. At the time, she was also banished thirteen miles from Telegraph Creek. This place was abandoned by previous Tahltan members. It was simply called Tahltan.

We lived at the mercy of other Tahltan members for moose meat, which was a necessity in our diets. On the plus side, mom planted a rather large garden. We were not short on vegetables, as we also had a root cellar in which storage for vegetables came in handy for use in winter. Basically, we were classified as subsistence farmers.

Raising a family without basic food was impossible. At the time, we didn't qualify for Indian Affairs' rations, which were given to all members on reserve. Mom was automatically taken off the Indian status list, being married to a white man, but she refused to be blackmailed into taking her children off the status list.

The Indian Affairs used this as a way to get us in their school. With threats of cutting off rations and the promise of a job in the same school, she relented. Once more, the government had accomplished their goal of putting more Natives in residential schools.

My brothers and I were part of the first fifteen students to enter Lower Post Indian residential school in September of 1951. Out of that group, four students graduated. One can argue that four out of fifteen is a terrific percentage, but of those four, three were my brothers and me. I had the easiest part in graduating, all I had to do was to follow my brothers' examples.

Over the years, I heard no mention of Mom's part in our success in graduating. Her attitude was something to behold. She always believed in our abilities to be successful in school and life. I am thankful, and I was proud to graduate with the second-highest average, with her being present at the reception. I look back and I can say that the proudest person at that ceremony was Mom. She stood 5′2 but that day, stood over everyone else present. Tears of joy streamed down her face as I was given my diploma. As far as I know, my brothers and I were three out of four to graduate from that particular school for twenty years.

Thank you, Mom. Did we graduate because of the residential system? I say we graduated in spite of the system, because students couldn't wait until their sixteenth birthday to get released. Speaking for myself, as I mentioned previously, I followed my two brothers' examples. Their graduation paved the way for me. I had every intention of quitting school after completing grade 10. My mother's influence had a major part in my decision to continue on to grade 11 and eventually graduate. Here again, I must thank her for the undying support and belief in her sons to step up a notch and persist to the end.

MOTHER

M is for her multitude of love

O is for options she gave

T is for her tenderness

H is for the heart she possessed

E is for every fibre of energy

R is for remembrance

To my mother, whose relentless love and understanding helped me through years of confinement in Canada's holocaust.

dads grad, dads grad with mother and sisters

Chapter Seventeen: From the Inside

Throughout the years, many stories have been told about residential abuse. A lot of them were studies by people who didn't experience firsthand the negative incidents that happened to Native children all over Canada and the United States. These studies are told from the outside looking in. My writing is genuine and told from the inside looking out.

We mostly looked out for freedom from confinement and religious persecution. Persecution, because our beliefs, and what they classify as "savage" methods, were beaten out of most of us. So they thought! Not being allowed to speak or talk about Native language was a priority. I ask you, who were the "savages?" Did we come from parents who beat children to teach language and the basics of life? They should have sat up and taken notice of Native teachings. Maybe then, more graduates would have come from residential schools. That would have defeated the reasons for those institutions.

Education was the furthest goal from their minds. After all, what good is an educated Indian? It was meant for us to remain dependant on the white society for all needs. Sixteen was the magic year most brothers and sisters chose to leave those prison-like atmospheres for a life of alcohol and drugs. If we continued, then the likelihood of major changes was more prevalent. Keeping us ignorant and dependant was more a priority.

Schools like that were kept open because of attendance. If our parents were given more opportunities to support a family, the residential era would never have happened. As it was, the last residential school survived into the 1990s. Now that Natives are learning how education is necessary, the Canadian society benefits also. After all, this is our country too. Canadians, as a whole, brag about being multicultural, but they forget the first inhabitants play an integral role in society and its success. Without our input and ideas, something is missing. Missing because our culture and beliefs are necessary in Canadian culture. We are an asset rather than a liability. I am only one of many whose life can thrive without alcohol or drugs. A clear mind and healthy body serve a better purpose in everyday life. In this family, our children don't have to think twice about graduating.

Priorities must be set and adhered to for progress in life to go on. A successful person is unfortunately judged by finances, rather than by the type of person he or she is. To achieve that end, we must continue to educate them and try to remain as our ancestors were. Pretty tall order, but it is a reality we must face.

Living in a white society does not mean isolation on reserves. I believe reserves have no purpose except to point out we are still captives of a superior society. To achieve that we have to live side by side and not be put up in a corner called a reserve. What better chance do we have at success than by living and fitting into society? I have faith and know we will prevail in joint efforts, as illustrated by our family. To fit in, one has to live with and deal with societal problems.

Our children, and I say this with pride, are excellent examples. They can have friends over anytime and not worry about parties to disrupt and ruin any activities planned. They can also spend times at friends' homes and are welcome anytime. It works both ways. If we were situated on a reserve, these activities would prove to be almost impossible. Reserve atmospheres do not cater to children of different ethnicities and backgrounds mingling. Although times are changing, the unfortunate fact on our reserve is the amount of alcohol and drugs used. Faced with this truth, people on reserves, I'm sure, are reluctant to host children in their homes, except for children from the same reserve, usually a relative. Society, I'm sure for good reason, is also reluctant to send a child into an atmosphere not up to standards. Put bluntly, we do not put our children's health at risk, nor lives in danger. We can't blame anyone for protecting children. After all, we also protect our loved ones. Would we send them to a violent household? That certainly would be putting their lives in danger.

With changing times, my hope is to blend Natives and whites as one. In the hereafter, our colour and creed will not matter to the Creator. What will count is the way we've led our lives on earth. Treating each other with respect is an excellent way to live out our existence. That would prove peaceful co-existence without prejudice. What a wonderful thought for future generations to follow.

We can all do our part by not judging others. We should be thankful for what we have, not dwell on the fact that there will always be someone who has more than we do. It is human nature to try to outdo our neighbour's wealth, but is it worth the effort. Look in the mirror and judge not. What you see is what you get. We can spend our whole lives wishing, but why when we can do something about our existence by ourselves? The person you see counts, not one who has the assets or money you want.

Children of all races pattern their futures after heroes. Why can't you be that idol?! If we close our eyes to bettering ourselves, then we are doing the same to our children. One does not need 20/20 vision to analyse lifestyles. Our children are too important because they are reflections of parents twenty to thirty years in the future. We can better ourselves without prejudice and hatred. Just because we've experienced all those negative feelings in past years is no excuse to pass them on to our children.

To move forward, we do not have to forget. Rather, we should remember and correct all those aspects that we have found to be negative. If we follow these simple rules, then the ones to benefit will be future generations. We, as parents, will also benefit and feel good about the improvements made in life's activities.

Pressure

Sometimes its easy to forget
The person within us
It's too easy to regret
Just like waiting for a late bus
What has happened
To leave us saddened

The words to describe
Are hard to come by
Do we need pills to help us die?
Therein comes the lie
Whatever life has in store
For us is something too pure

My life of booze is over
Now I have my boys
They are my inspiration forever
Now I have my boys
I have thought about death
I will not let that be my threat

Chapter Eighteen: After Effects

I was recently watching a TV show where they discussed a survey on molested children. The topic was that the victims had to wait a minimum of three months before any professional help was initiated. This statement brings my thoughts back fifty years plus, in that First Nations had to wait to receive any form of help in that aspect. The program went on to say that three months is too long to wait for help in getting these kids back on the right track for normal living. The devastating effect this wait has on the minds of children is too much. The program concluded that the long wait can permanently damage them, maybe for life. We can focus on modern-day cases of molesting, and through Health Canada get these kids assistance as soon as possible. If this is true, then the children deserve all forms of medical advice available.

If time affects the outcomes of recovery, then what about the extremely long wait we as victims of residential school abuse had to endure? We were molested in the worst possible way. Not only were we denied help, but in most cases, there was total denial that these abuses ever happened. By the time help became available, most of us had wasted lives by being total alcoholics or drug addicts, sometimes both. I must ask, in all honesty, what is the proper procedure in restoring us back to normal human beings? How do you enter a mind after all those years of total neglect and denial? Those who are guilty must own up to any and all acts of disgust they initiated. I've not heard anyone guilty assuring us that we had no part in the inhumane treatments inflicted upon us so many years ago. I would like to hear them say, "I am totally responsible, and you had no way to stop any actions taken on your bodies." That is a pretty far-fetched statement. I believe this would be a giant step towards recovery. After all, can we compare three months of neglected treatment to thirty to fifty years of total silence? Is it any wonder that we turned to alternate means to wipe out memories of our childhood years? Memories, I might add, that should be cherished, not blocked out.

The erasing of those memories caused a lot of turmoil in Native communities. Turmoil that has progressed so far that we have a difficult time dealing and coping, to heal. First Nations were looked on as drunks and people who couldn't accomplish goals in life. We didn't have the capabilities to face life head-on. Any failure on our part was magnified in comparison to other Canadians and was always the main topic of discussion. If ownership was accountable years ago, then our people would have had a better chance to change.

According to surveys, immediate help is essential to the wellbeing of victims. The devastating effects of residential schools on First Nations is something that cannot be put in words. A person has to experience abuse to be able to talk about the past. I, for one, think that the best way to handle these cases is not impossible. The obvious person to approach for answers are the victims. Victims, because we know exactly what our brothers and sisters have gone through.

When that person says, "I understand and know how you feel," we will know that statement has viable input. Treatment coming from that person would hold more meaning as opposed to a university graduate who has studied the situation. We have people of First Nations descent, whose capabilities and backgrounds fit in that category. When all is said and done, I'm sure we, as a nation, will benefit in a more positive way and heal faster.

We look at the teacher and visualize because of their nationality, as the ones who molested us in the first place. That is only human nature. I look into the future and see all teachers and therapists coming from our own communities. We need teachers, etc., who not only know First Nations, but also who understand our lifestyles and traditions. Who better than a person coming from the community? It is one thing to study our culture, another to live and breathe the same air. Our problems and addictions stem from white people's abuse on both our body and mind. Don't blame a Native for being suspicious of a white person telling them they understand and have the solution to patch up our problems. We, as a nation, now have numerous teachers who have the capability to pass on their knowledge. They will assist in the healing process, which is needed now. Time is of essence as the saying goes.

The knowledge we've achieved living in the residential systems can now be passed on to younger First Nations. The truth and answers will come as we talk amongst each other. Right or wrong, it will be truthful. We don't have to guess about problems we face. Conversation about our past experiences is a healing process in itself. Solutions will follow automatically. The best teachers are the ones who have lived and survived to communicate.

The road to healing is within our grasp. We are on the right path, but to achieve, we have to not only dream but initiate. Results will follow according to what methods are used. We now have the solution in our backyard. Reach out and take advantage to move forward, led by First Nations. We do have the knowledge and the answer. To justify, we have to rectify.

The punishment we received by use of the strap was only one method I've witnessed or become a part of. In addition to all the beatings I've witnessed or became a part of, I recall the punishment of watching my Native brothers' strapping. Horrifying. I put myself in their place and seemed to absorb the pain in my mind. I made a pledge: this will never happen to me. Obedience seemed to come easier. Everything I was told to do was enjoyment, was a necessity. I even told this particular person that I wasn't afraid because I enjoyed whatever was done to me. The public strapping became less as time progressed. It was as if all of us had finally become a part of their regime.

The supervisor had a major part in our silence. His punishment was on human endurance. If anyone disobeyed, then all the boys were punished. We ran around the gym at a slow pace. The only obstacles were benches two feet to two-and-a-half feet high. They were placed approximately fifteen feet apart. Pretty easy task you might say, but after two hours we faded. Another endurance test consisted of kneeling on the cement floor with both arms held above the head. It, again, was easy at first. Our arms and shoulders would become numb. After the numbness, pain follows. Push-ups were added to those who dared to drop their arms. I can say with clarity that doing push-ups after holding your arms up for an indefinite time is next to impossible. I've witnessed boys crying out in pain because they could take anymore.

No human consideration was taken in their methods of discipline. We as human beings had to go through life raising children with these backgrounds as credentials. Some of us, myself included, could not settle down until the age of forty to begin raising a family. It was extremely difficult not to pass on residential treatment to my kids, whom I love with a capitol "L." I can't deny that my temper got the best of me at first. It was taken out on my children. I now only have to think about the treatment I received as a child and the results. We, as tots, were beaten and leant to obey through those methods. The problem with this is easy to explain but hard to correct.

A child who is slapped or disciplined with a strap will only listen when those methods are used. What happens when we stop because children eventually grow up? They become as we did years ago. As our sixteenth birthday approached, we were free to do as we pleased. Maybe to inflict damage on someone else.

This became a reality when wives became a target of husbands who tried to force them to be at their bidding for everything. Even the laws at that time seemed to cater to the husband. Charges were laid and more often than not dropped by wives. When this happened, the law had no choice but to drop charges too. Our female population had nowhere to turn or any organizations to join for comfort. Organizations, which aided in accessing, and hopefully solving, family problems. These types have become less prevalent, but some still exist.

We, as Native brothers and sisters, must first of all set a good example and then be willing to talk about the problems we face. Workshops are the ideal place to attend to converse and pass on this knowledge to the public who are willing to listen. Hearing this from a First Nations person is a step in the right direction, especially if the third party wants to listen and also speak about all problems. After all, their problems are mutually ours too. Problems that are discussed together are also solved as one. When we talk about mutual problems, we eventually will find an avenue to pursue. That avenue will hopefully lead to an answer and solution to problems faced by First Nations nationwide.

The future doesn't hold answers; the present is here now waiting for solutions. If we wait for the future, our children will face the same fears we had, with no aspirations. Aspirations to face and solve our difficulties in Native ways with sweathouses and large gatherings as honouring the dead. Attending a sweathouse brings out the true Native souls and inner beliefs in life. It cleanses the soul and mind and actually seems to rectify all the wrongs done to us and Natives from days gone by. Washing the guilt from the mind is a major step on the long road to recovery.

Everything we do in life has a meaning, from the smallest incident to the final hours we spend on this here Mother Earth.

Future

I focus on the future
The lights are bright
I focus on the future
I've set the facts right
The past is gone
Days are now not forlorn

The future looks bright
I hope I'm right
Opening up the future
Looking back in time
Keeping myself in line

The forsaken are not forgotten
Only put on hold
The forsaken are not forgotten
Lo and behold
The light shines brighter ahead
Let us think of the future instead

all boys grad with dad, Albert's future goal was
to get his boys to finish school like he did

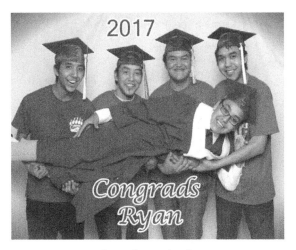

boys done school

ROSA

The setting sun does no justice
The early morning dawn does more
Of all the rainbows in the heavenly sky
Your smile gives more radiance
I dreamt about this moment
Of this I have to comment

I've lived through the annals of time
I've lived through periods of sublime
But never thought my time would come
That the world would stand still
And all my troubles would dissolve
As it did that day of resolve

Your radiance brightened up the room
Your smile became a fixture in my mind
I wanted this moment to last
I seemed to forget the past
I was smitten like a dove
Because of thee I love

I have one thing to say
I love you more each day
We always have our disagreements
We always have our arguments
But as time passes, I must say
I love you more each day

God Restores the Broken Vessel

Pastor from Prince Rupert B.C.
Albert Etzerza's Memorial Service.
January 4, 2019
Dease Lake, B.C.

Isaiah 30:14
And He shall break it like the breaking of a potter's vessel, which is broken to pieces; he shall not spare. So, there shall not be found among its broken pieces, a piece big enough to take hot coals from the fireplace nor big enough to take water from the creek.

Psalm 55:6-8 I said, "Oh, that I had wings of a dove! I would fly away and be at rest. Indeed I would wander far off and remain in the wilderness; I would speed up my escape from the windy storm and tempest."

Ecclesiastics 9:10
Whatever your hands find to do, do it with all your might, for out of the realm of the dead, where you are going, there is neither working nor planning nor knowledge or wisdom.

Today we come to celebrate the life of Albert Etzerza: Now I would like to briefly share with you the above scriptures, and they all had to do with our past life. Where I met Bert (or Albert or Berdie) was in our residential school and this is how we identified him, besides his number, which may have been 7. I think the brothers were 6,7 and 8, if I am not mistaken.

The Bible tells us that when God created us that he created us in His image, meaning that when we went into the residential school, we were innocent and beautiful human beings. Natives believe that there is a creator. However, in the process, man was trying to mould us in his own religious image and shattered and destroyed a beautiful vessel in the process.

In 1951, Bert was put into the residential school at six years old, and that is when the potter's vessel started to break into pieces.

Not only his heart was broken, but what carried the heart of the whole man was broken, his spirit, soul, and body. Gradually he was being broken down to little bits, piece-by-piece, until he was shattered into disrepair. The potter's vessel was broken. Another eagle lost his wings.

After that, being in a broken condition, he tried to fly the best he could, and he tried to fly with broken wings for the longest time. Like myself and so many others who had experienced this trauma, all he wanted to do at first was to run and hide and just get as far away from our past as possible.

Like the Psalmist said, "Oh, if I had the wings of a dove, I would fly away from this storm."

However, Bert just didn't lie down and give up, because, in the original Bert, the Creator gave him great talents and ability and intelligence to accomplish great and wonderful things. With broken wings and a partly broken spirit, he arose out of the ashes to push himself with all his might. He pushed himself and got an education, and whatever he did, he did with all his might. He pushed himself out of the ashes of despair and repaired his broken wings to fly again.

I don't know how many years that Bert ran from his storm before he found the love of his life and she became his sunshine, Rosa. I believe that she was the one that finally calmed his storm through the sons that they had together, and she was probably that one sent to save what remained of a most wonderful man's life.

You see, behind all this brokenness of Albert and our Tahltan people and others is, the Lord loved him to send someone to love him. Well, our Creator, as we call him; his name is Jesus Christ. He was sent from the Father to us also, to show us his love, show us the way, the truth, and the life and that no one comes to the Father except through him.

Jesus Christ was the one who showed love to humanity. He suffered, he was crucified and died on the cruel cross, and on the third day, He rose again. He gave His life to be God over the Tahltan people and the whole world. Do you ever think why God put the Tahltan people at the head of three main rivers? God has a plan for His people if they would come to him. Let us pray.

Albert Etzerza

Albert Remembered: A Tribute by His Sons

My pops meant the world to me, always told stories of his life, good and bad; we never got tired of his stories.

I travelled with him to court, to Whitehorse, then he got us all in hockey. The Montreal Canadiens, his team. We made it to the top by copying their plays.

His favourite thing was hockey, which made us all love it more, and watching it with my pops was just the best. As long as we had food and a roof over our head, he did not care about anything else.

But he never gave up, and with five boys to feed and a wife to look after, he did great.

Family came first, no matter what!

We never saw him drink, all though he called himself an alcoholic. "It only takes one drink," he said.

But my dad was my best friend, brother, and *father*. He's gone but is still looking after us.

-Graham

My father means a lot to me. I spent a lot of time with him in the end—hospital trips, doctor appointments—nonetheless, I was more than happy to be with my dad almost every step of his way to heaven. I was once asked the hardest question of my life, and that was from my father. He asked me if it was okay to give up. He said he's tired and he misses his mom, and he knows that we're all good. He got to witness a miracle in front of his own eyes. He got to witness all his children graduate—some struggles, but the confidence and willpower and determination gets you through anything.

My father has given us the best tool for life, and that's to always work hard and provide for your family, no matter what. He was one legged and still carried us as babies somehow, cooked for us, and drove us to school and around Terrace to trick-or-treat. He couldn't do much with us, but yet, he still did everything; couldn't play sports with us, but he played games; couldn't play outside with us but watched anything we wanted with us. He didn't like wrestling at all (WWE) but still turned off NHL (his most favourite sport in the world) so we kids could watch our wrestling, even during playoff time. Now NHL is my go to!

I'm happy my father helped me graduate and taught me what he did, all the cooking skills and manners and how to love and care for a woman and treat her. Thank you, father, Albert, my dad. God bless you and RIP.

-Evan

November 3, 2020

I've grown more to the realization that I bear the name of my passing father, Albert Henry Etzerza as Albert Henry Etzerza Junior; and although I know that makes me no different than my brothers, it makes me proud to be the son of such a story. To be the son of Albert Etzerza was more than a blessing. He always made sure that we had what we needed as children growing up and went above and beyond to ensure it. An everlasting memory to be imprinted in my heart; the way he treated our family with such kindness and love will forever stay with me. My father was one of the smartest people I knew; he always made it clear how important schooling is to my future and that my efforts in whatever I am to do, play an important role in who I am as a person. I truly believe all of my dad's teachings, as my brothers and I grew, were simply passed onto us and will remain with us for eternity.

With that being said, not a day goes by that I don't think of my father. He was resilient, hard working, and a caring and loving man. I truly believe this is a story to be read, learnt, and passed on, as it tells the truth behind such a dark era for Native culture. The words are written precisely to leave you in a train of thought like no other. Love you, Papa, Dad, and my hero.

-Albert Henry

My dad was courageous. After everything he had been through, he was able to take care of Mom and, most importantly, us children. He had an ability that I could never dream of having. He never gave up on his dream; even with his disability, he was able to carry us to our rooms when we were kids. His speech was on point, in my opinion. Everything I learnt was from him. He never broke a sweat, only when cooking because it got hot in there. Dad was the person who made me feel like home, but before he passed he told me to stay strong no matter what.

I love you, Dad.

-Brandon

My Father, Albert Etzerza, was my best friend growing up in my life. He was always there for me when I needed him and has taught me everything I know. He's the one who showed me what hockey was, and it grew to be my favourite thing to watch, and even play. His favourite team was the Montreal Canadiens, which is mine, and all of my brother's, favourite team. Watching hockey was my dad's favourite thing to do, besides hanging out with any of his family members. Playoff time was probably his favourite time just because he got to hang out with all of us and watch the Canadiens play.

My father has told me countless stories about his life growing up, and I can remember most of them, but he never told me about his time in residential school, at least not going into as much detail as this, but reading this has taught me that no matter what happens in your life, you can overcome anything you believe in. In memory of my father, I have gotten a memorial Tattoo on my right arm of the Montreal Canadiens logo with his initials on it. He may have never approved of tattoos, but I'm sure he would have approved of this. I love you, Dad, so much, and I miss you every day.

-Ryan

kissing cup, life time Montreal fan an his boys fallowed

dad with his cake

dad's cake, birthdays were celebrated
with nothing but Montreal logs

first of all natives to take them to court,
and made others to come forword

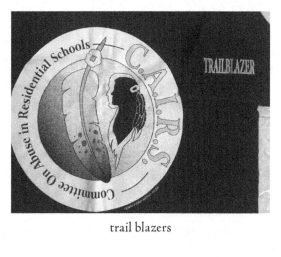

trail blazers

Made in the USA
Monee, IL
06 February 2021

59773943R00066